Chinese Zodiac Animals

Copyright © 2012 Shanghai Press and Publishing Development Company

This book is edited and designed by the Editorial Committee of *Cultural China* series

Managing Directors: Wang Youbu, Xu Naiqing
Editorial Director: Wu Ying
Editors: Yang Xiaohe, Ginley Regencia

Story and Illustrations: Sanmu Tang
Translation by Zhu Jingwen

ISBN: 978-1-60220-977-0

Address any comments about *Chinese Zodiac Animals* to:

Better Link Press
99 Park Ave
New York, NY 10016
USA

or

Shanghai Press and Publishing Development Company
F 7 Donghu Road, Shanghai, China (200031)
Email: comments_betterlinkpress@hotmail.com

Printed in China by Shanghai Donnelley Printing Co., Ltd.

1 3 5 7 9 10 8 6 4 2

Chinese Zodiac Animals

By Sanmu Tang

Better Link Press

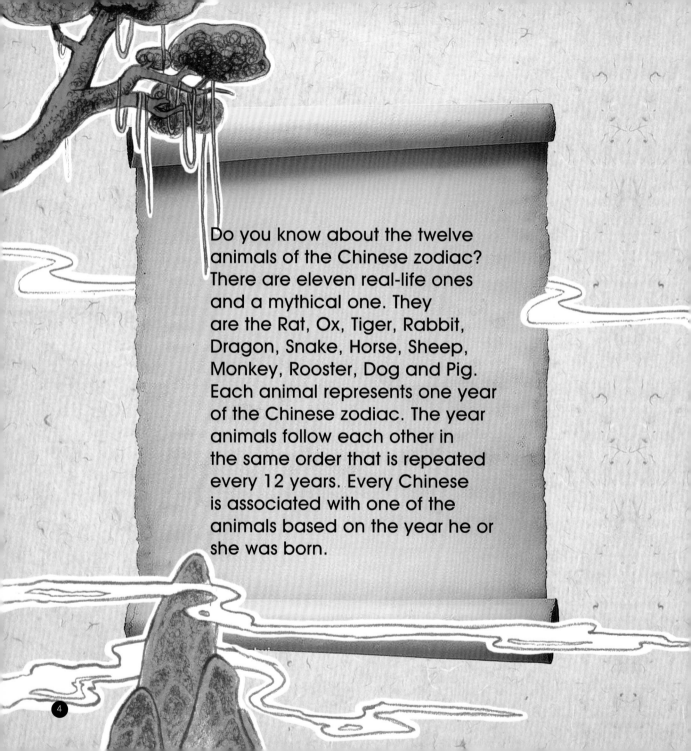

Do you know about the twelve animals of the Chinese zodiac? There are eleven real-life ones and a mythical one. They are the Rat, Ox, Tiger, Rabbit, Dragon, Snake, Horse, Sheep, Monkey, Rooster, Dog and Pig. Each animal represents one year of the Chinese zodiac. The year animals follow each other in the same order that is repeated every 12 years. Every Chinese is associated with one of the animals based on the year he or she was born.

The practice of using the twelve animals to mark each year of the calendar started long ago in China. Over time, people started being identified closely with their birth year animal. People started to believe that someone's personality and fate were influenced by his or her animal sign. What's your Chinese zodiac sign? What does it say about you? Let's take a look.

鼠 The Clever and Affluent Rat

The first sign of the Chinese zodiac represents resourcefulness and wealth.

People born in the year of
the Rat are cheerful and
direct by nature.

Their sharp instincts make
them good strategists.

Females born in the year of the Rat are
clever and bright, and can manage both
their families and lives pretty well.

They are very capable but
can be impatient for quick
results.

Choice of Profession

A positive outlook and independent nature makes Rats suitable for work that lets them express their individuality such as scholarly research, teaching or writing.

Advice

They need to be more open to other people's opinions and guard against overconfidence.

Money Matters

Thrifty by nature, the Rat's nest egg ensures a stable and comfortable life.

Feb. 5, 1924 ~ Jan 24, 1925	Jan 24, 1936 ~ Feb. 10, 1937	Feb.10, 1948 ~ Jan. 28, 1949
Jan. 28, 1960 ~ Feb. 14, 1961	Feb. 15, 1972 ~ Feb 2, 1973	Feb. 2, 1984 ~ Feb. 19, 1985
Feb.19, 1996 ~ Feb. 6, 1997	Feb. 6, 2008 ~ Jan. 25, 2009	Jan. 25, 2020 ~ Feb. 11, 2021

Who do Rats best get along with?

Lucky Color

Shades of blue— symbolizing wisdom and ideals

牛 The Honest and Down-to-earth Ox

The second sign of the Chinese zodiac is steadfast and patient.

They are deep thinkers and are always conscientious, but the Ox is also stubborn.

People born in the year of the Ox are considered honest, diligent and dependable. These qualities will win them the appreciation and trust of their bosses.

They are patient and persevering and are usually late-bloomers.

They can become ferocious and dangerous as an untamed ox when angry. It would be wise for others to keep their distance.

Advice

Those born in the year of the Ox tend to rely on their own advice. They can be rather inflexible and prone to extremism. They need to keep their temper under control and be open-minded.

Choice of Profession

The most satisfying jobs for these hardworking and dedicated people are doctor, journalist, lawyer, civil servant, office worker, and social worker.

Money Matters

The responsible Ox manages his money carefully and will be prosperous.

YEARS OF BIRTH

Jan. 25, 1925
~
Feb.12, 1926

Feb. 11, 1937
~
Jan.30, 1938

Jan.29, 1949
~
Feb. 16, 1950

Feb. 15, 1961
~
Feb. 4, 1962

Feb. 3, 1973
~
Jan. 22, 1974

Feb. 20, 1985
~
Feb. 8, 1986

Feb. 7, 1997
~
Jan. 27, 1998

Jan. 26, 2009
~
Feb. 13, 2010

Feb. 12, 2021
~
Jan. 31, 2022

 Who do Oxen best get along with?

Lucky Color

Shades of black—symbolizing responsibility and courage

15

虎 The Adventurous Tiger

The third sign of the Chinese zodiac represents justice and courage.

People born in the year of the Tiger are independent and fearless. They often rush to the forefront of whatever they do.

They are cheerful and eager to lend a helping hand.

They have a strong sense of justice and will stand up for what they feel is righteous.

From time to time their tendency to act in haste without proper consideration can lead them to failure.

Advice

Tigers will experience many ups and downs in their lifetime, so they need to prepare for the rainy days. Maintaining a positive outlook will also help Tigers to overcome difficulties.

Choice of Profession

Nothing is impossible for Tigers. They are able to excel in their chosen fields and be recognized for their achievements. They will find success as CEOs, adventurers, politicians, policemen, designers and actors.

Money Matters

For greater success, passionate Tigers should practice self-control when it comes to handling money and finances.

Feb. 13, 1926
~
Feb. 1 1927

Jan. 31, 1938
~
Feb. 18, 1939

Feb. 17, 1950
~
Feb. 5, 1951

Feb. 5, 1962
~
Jan. 24, 1963

Jan. 23, 1974
~
Feb. 10, 1975

Feb. 9, 1986
~
Jan. 28, 1987

Jan. 28, 1998
~
Feb. 15, 1999

Feb. 14, 2010
~
Feb. 2, 2011

Feb. 1, 2022
~
Jan. 21, 2023

 Who do Tigers best get along with?

Lucky Color

Shades of olive or grass green—symbolizing nature and peace

兔 The Refined and Astute Rabbit

The fourth sign of the Chinese zodiac symbolizes quick wit and virtue.

The peace loving Rabbit is always polite and well-mannered.

Beneath their calm façade lies a restless heart. They are strong-willed people and do not like to be held back.

They like to show off sometimes and are fashion-conscious.

They treat their children kindly and gently, but with discipline. They will never be too indulgent or show favoritism toward one child.

Advice

Rabbits can be overly sensitive and tend to think too much. This can cause them unnecessary frustrations in dealing with people. They need to learn to put things in perspective.

Choice of Profession

Ideal jobs for the Rabbit include writer, painter, musician, architect, consultant and translator; all require attention to detail and shrewd observation.

Money Matters

Rabbits are generally lucky when it comes to finances. Their generous and easy-going natures seem to increase their chances of getting rich.

YEARS OF BIRTH

Feb. 2, 1927
~
Jan. 22, 1928

Feb. 19, 1939
~
Feb. 7, 19401940

Feb. 6, 1951
~
Jan. 26, 1952

Jan. 25, 1963
~
Feb. 12, 1964

Feb. 11, 1975
~
Jan. 30, 1976

Jan. 29, 1987
~
Feb. 16, 1988

Feb. 16, 1999
~
Feb. 4, 2000

Feb. 3, 2011
~
Jan. 22, 2012

Jan. 22, 2023
~
Jan. 29, 2024

 Who do Rabbits best get along with?

Lucky Color

Shades of purple—symbolizing mystery and charisma

The Most Impressive Dragon

The fifth sign of the Chinese zodiac symbolizes determination and strength.

People born in the year of the mystical Dragon are dazzling and exotic. They go after what they want and nothing deters them.

They are broad-minded, big-hearted and forgiving. They are genuinely appealing to others and have a natural authority.

Fortified by inner strength, they are extremely brave.

Their extraordinary talent can make them arrogant, overambitious and impulsive.

Advice

They should learn to be more patient and remember to finish what they start.

Choice of Profession

Noble Dragons have lofty ideals and need to strive for a cause. They are well-suited to being directors, lawyers, brokers and entrepreneurs.

Money Matters

Dragons can easily make and lose lots of money. But they should not let temporary setbacks get them down and should focus on retaining wealth.

Jan. 23, 1928
~
Feb. 9, 1929

Feb. 8, 1940
~
Jan. 26, 1941

Jan. 27, 1952
~
Feb. 13, 1953

Feb. 13, 1964
~
Feb. 1, 1965

Jan. 31, 1976
~
Feb. 17, 1977

Feb. 17, 1988
~
Feb. 5, 1989

Feb. 5, 2000
~
Jan. 23, 2001

Jan. 23, 2012
~
Feb. 9, 2013

Feb. 10, 2024
~
Jan. 28, 2025

Who do Dragons best get along with?

Lucky Color

Shades of orange and yellow—symbolizing tact and worldliness.

蛇 The Secretive Snake

The sixth sign of the Chinese zodiac symbolizes virtue and outward calm.

They can sometimes be suspicious. When meeting someone new, they tend to keep their distance for their own protection, but once the initial suspicion is overcome, they will become the most thoughtful and considerate friends.

People born in the year of the Snake are intelligent and composed.

Snakes always plan ahead. They are organized and decisive in reaching goals they set for themselves.

They greatly appreciate beauty and the finest things.

Advice

Intelligent Snakes are effective at getting what they want but should be careful not to become overly ambitious and greedy.

Choice of Profession

They will do better in jobs where they can use their brains. These include statesman, financier, philosopher, psychiatrist or public relations agent.

Money Matters

They are very lucky with money, always finding more if they need it.

YEARS OF BIRTH

Feb. 10, 1929 ~ Jan. 29, 1930	Jan. 27, 1941 ~ Feb. 14, 1942	Feb. 14, 1953 ~ Feb. 2, 1954
Feb. 2, 1965 ~ Jan. 20, 1966	Feb. 18, 1977 ~ Feb. 6, 1978	Feb. 6, 1989 ~ Jan. 26, 1990
Jan. 24, 2001 ~ Feb. 11, 2002	Feb. 10, 2013 ~ Jan. 30, 2014	Jan. 29, 2025 ~ Feb. 16, 2026

 Who do Snakes best get along with?

Lucky Color

Shades of off-white and white—symbolizing truthfulness and perfection

馬 The Independent and Spontaneous Horse

The seventh sign of the Chinese zodiac represents passion and agility.

People born in the year of the Horse do not like to admit defeat without a fight. They always strive to do their best.

They are honest, direct and vivacious. They get along with others easily and have no problem finding help when needed.

Impulsive and willful at times, they can severely underestimate the challenges that will come their way.

They are quick-witted and easily come up with answers.

Advice

Horses need to be more patient. They need to learn to stay the course and not leave things halfway done.

will power

endurance

Choice of Profession

Because of their innate self-confidence, Horses can wwbe adventurers, architects, salesmen, artists, entrepreneurs or scientists. Such jobs tap their talent and let them freely express themselves.

Money Matters

They make and spend fortunes easily. Horses have expensive tastes and will end up with little savings.

YEARS OF BIRTH

Jan. 30, 1930
~
Feb. 16, 1931

Feb. 15, 1942
~
Feb. 4, 1943

Feb. 3, 1954
~
Jan. 23, 1955

Jan. 21, 1966
~
Feb. 8, 1967

Feb. 7, 1978
~
Jan. 27, 1979

FJan. 27, 1990
~
Feb. 14, 1991

Feb. 11, 2002
~
Jan. 31, 2003

Jan. 31, 2014
~
Feb. 18, 2015

Feb. 16, 2026
~
Feb. 5, 2027

Who do Horses best get along with?

Lucky Color

Shades of gold—symbolizing respectability and generosity

羊 The Docile and Compassionate Sheep

The eighth sign of the Chinese zodiac symbolizes obedience and kindness.

They are selfless and easily touched by the misfortune of others.

People born in the year of the Sheep are sensitive, prudent and upright.

The Sheep can seem pessimistic and be a worrier. They tend to resign themselves to fate and don't like to be stuck with routines.

Beneath the Sheep's mild exterior lies an inner strength. They are able to protect themselves when needed.

Advice

They are not good at handling setbacks and frustrations. They need to learn to be tougher and stronger.

Money Matters

Their giving natures make them poor money managers. But they still are able to lead a stable life without want thanks to help from friends.

Choice of Profession

The highly creative Sheep will find rewarding work in art, advertising, public service, the beauty business, consulting and social services.

YEARS OF BIRTH

Feb. 17, 1931 ~ Feb. 5, 1932	Feb. 5, 1943 ~ Jan. 24, 1944	Jan. 24, 1955 ~ Feb. 11, 1956
Feb. 9, 1967 ~ Jan. 29, 1968	Jan. 28, 1979 ~ Feb. 15, 1980	Feb. 15, 1991 ~ Feb. 3, 1992
Feb. 1, 2003 ~ Jan. 21, 2004	Feb. 19, 2015 ~ Feb. 7, 2016	Feb. 6, 2027 ~ Jan. 25, 2028

 Who do Sheep best get along with?

Lucky Color

Shades of silver—
symbolizing gentleness
and tolerance

39

猴 The Vibrant and Quick-witted Monkey

The ninth sign of the Chinese zodiac represents intelligence and liveliness.

People born under the sign of the Monkey are humorous, clever and cannot sit still. They are charming and popular.

Energetic Monkeys love life and are multi-talented.

Playful Monkeys don't like being told what to do. They would prefer to live a carefree life.

silence

Even from an early age, Monkeys have great memories and can remember a lot. To other people though, they can seem shallow and absentminded.

Advice

Caring too much about fame and fortune may be their weakness; vanity may lead to their downfall.

Choice of Profession

They will find success if they take the time to choose a field that truly interests them. Work in diplomacy, social advocacy, law, performing arts and sports may suit them.

Money Matters

Outgoing Monkeys will have many opportunities to make their fortune. They can go far if they manage their money well.

YEARS OF BIRTH

Feb. 6, 1932 ~ Jan. 25, 1933	Jan. 25, 1944 ~ Feb. 12, 1945	Feb. 12, 1956 ~ Jan. 30, 1957
Jan. 30, 1968 ~ Feb. 16, 1969	Feb. 16, 1980 ~ Feb. 4, 1981	Feb. 4, 1992 ~ Jan. 22, 1993
Jan. 22, 2004 ~ Feb. 8, 2005	Feb. 8, 2016 ~ Jan. 27, 2017	Jan. 26, 2028 ~ Feb. 12, 2029

 Who do Monkeys best get along with?

Lucky Color

Shades of yellow—symbolizing curiosity and change

43

雞 The Dashing Rooster

The tenth sign of the Chinese zodiac symbolizes carefulness and decisiveness.

People born in the year of the Rooster are motivated creatures who quickly respond to solve all kinds of problems.

The clear-sighted Rooster is organized and precise. They pay much attention when they work.

They are extremely social and prefer to be the center of attention.

Vanity and being too demanding are their biggest shortcomings.

Advice

Picky Roosters should refrain from nagging their families and their staff when they don't meet their high expectations.

Choice of Profession

They are good at handling money and do well in finance-related jobs like accounting, bookkeeping, or statistics. They are good entrepreneurs.

Money Matters

Their skill at keeping budgets allows them to live without money worries.

Jan. 26, 1933 ~ Feb. 13, 1934	Feb. 13, 1945 ~ Feb. 1, 1946	Jan. 31, 1957 ~ Feb. 17, 1958
Feb. 17, 1969 ~ Feb. 5, 1970	Feb. 5, 1981 ~ Jan. 24, 1982	Jan. 23, 1993 ~ Feb. 9, 1994
Feb. 9, 2005 ~ Jan. 28, 2006	Jan. 28, 2017 ~ Feb. 15, 2018	Feb. 13, 2029 ~ Feb. 2, 2030

Who do Roosters best get along with?

Lucky Color

Shades of orange red—symbolizing wealth and resolve

狗 The Faithful and Honest Dog

The eleventh sign of the Chinese zodiac represents loyalty and dedication.

People born in the year of the Dog are genuine. All their emotions, be it happiness, anger, grief or joy can be seen on their faces.

They do not easily give their affection but when they do, they are your friend for life.

They are responsible and trustworthy. They have a strong sense of fair play, and show compassion for other people's troubles.

Beneath their cheerful exterior, Dogs tend to be constant worriers, seeing only the downside of things.

Advice

Stubborn and pessimistic Dogs are feared for their biting comments. They need to learn more rational conduct.

Money Matters

Dogs spend money wisely, and are destined to lead a life of abundance.

Choice of Profession

Their strong senses of duty suit them for working in the science and technology field. They make great architects, doctors, judges, lawyers, consultants, teachers and secretaries.

YEARS OF BIRTH

Feb. 14, 1934 ~ Feb. 3, 1935	Feb. 2, 1946 ~ Jan. 21, 1947	Feb. 18, 1958 ~ Feb. 7, 1959
Feb. 6, 1970 ~ Jan. 26, 1971	Jan. 25, 1982 ~ Feb. 12, 1983	Feb. 10, 1994 ~ Jan. 30, 1995
Jan. 29, 2006 ~ Feb. 17, 2007	Feb. 16, 2018 ~ Feb. 4, 2019	Feb. 3, 2030 ~ Jan. 22, 2031

 Who do Dogs best get along with?

Lucky Color

Shades of red—symbolizing passion and vitality

51

猪 The Generous and Considerate Pig

The last sign of the Chinese zodiac represents understanding and tolerance.

Those born in the year of the Pig believe in the basic goodness of people. They are honest and sincere.

Easy-going Pigs are fun to be around. They enjoy all kinds of social gatherings.

They have many friends because they never fail to treat others with warmth and respect.

Pigs are far too trusting. It can be easy for others to take advantage of them.

Advice

Their honest nature can make them tactless. They can offend others and sometimes get in trouble for being too blunt.

Choice of Profession

Hardworking Pigs are always willing to help out their colleagues at work. They are successful teachers and public servants.

Money Matters

The Pig is the luckiest among all the signs when it comes to finances. Though they love to spend, they also attract money to them. They may become rich at a young age.